CULTIVATING BEG
PLAN

Valid Step By Step Fundamental Guide For Newbie Begonia Flower Plant Gardeners

GREGORY SMITH

Table of Contents

Introductory

Begonia flowers are a variety of flowering plant in the family Begoniaceae. These flowers are renowned for their vivid and varied hues, distinct shapes, and ornamental foliage. Their aesthetic allure makes them popular choices for gardens, interior decoration, and landscaping.

The significance of begonia flowers can vary based on cultural and personal interpretations. In general, begonia flowers can represent the following sentiments:

• Begonias are frequently viewed as cheerful and happy flowers, and they can be given to convey happiness, appreciation, and gratitude.

• Sophistication and Elegance: The intricate and varied shapes of begonia flowers, along with their vibrant hues, can convey sophistication and elegance. They can be used to convey sophistication and good taste.

• Begonias can be exchanged between companions to represent comradery and the enduring bond of friendship.

• Perhaps due to the delicate nature of their blossoms, begonias are associated with caution and wariness in some cultures. This symbolism may derive from the notion that one must approach situations with caution.

• The balanced development and symmetry of begonia plants can be interpreted as a representation of equilibrium and harmony.

• Begonias are resilient plants that can flourish in a variety of environments. Consequently, they can represent resiliency, adaptability, and the capacity to thrive even in harsh environments.

Noting that flower meanings can be extremely subjective and culturally influenced is essential. Begonia flowers may carry varying significance for various societies and individuals.

If you are contemplating giving begonia flowers as a gift or using them in a particular context, it may be beneficial to consider the recipient's cultural background and personal preferences to ensure that the gesture is meaningful to them.

CHAPTER ONE
Begonia Vegetation Varieties

Begonias are a diverse group of plants that are available in numerous shapes, sizes, hues, and forms. They are classified according to their growth patterns, foliage characteristics, and flower varieties. Here are some prominent varieties of begonia:

• Tuberous Begonias (Begonia x tuberhybrida) are renowned for their colorful, large, and showy blossoms. They are available with single or double blossoms and a variety of hues. Commonly cultivated as annuals, tuberous begonias are frequently utilized in hanging baskets, containers, and garden beds.

• Rex Begonias (Begonia rex-cultorum): These begonias are appreciated for their remarkable foliage. The leaves can be intricate and multicolored, with patterns varying from spirals to swirls and frequently displaying silver, purple, red, and green hues. Rex begonias are typically grown indoors and are cultivated for their foliage.

• Fibrous-Rooted Begonias (Begonia semperflorens): Also referred to as bedding begonias, these plants are frequently used in landscaping due to their compact growth habit and continuous flowering. The flowers are tiny to medium in size and come in a variety of hues.

• Cane or Angel Wing Begonias (Begonia coccinea and others): These begonias have stems resembling bamboo and produce clusters of suspended flowers. The flowers can be pink, scarlet, or white, and the leaves resemble angel wings and are typically asymmetrical.

• Tuberous-Rooted Begonias (Begonia boliviensis): Similar to tuberous begonias, but with a trailing growth tendency. They are frequently used in hanging baskets and containers and produce orange, red, and pink tubular blossoms.

• Wax Begonias (Begonia x semperflorens-cultorum): These begonias are compact and bushy, with lustrous green or bronze foliage and small white, pink, or red flowers with a waxy texture.

They are frequently used as bedding plants and are valued for their adaptability to a variety of growing conditions.

• These begonias have dense, fleshy rhizomes and are cultivated primarily for their distinctive foliage.

Variable leaf shapes, sizes, and patterns make them popular among collectors. Begonia rex and Begonia maculata are examples of popular rhizomatous begonias.

• Due to their trailing growth tendency, trailing begonias are excellent for hanging baskets and containers. They produce small, delicate blossoms and are ideal for creating a cascading effect in your garden or interior space.

• Certain begonia species can be grown outdoors in temperate climates due to their hardiness. Begonia grandis and Begonia evansiana are examples. Typically, these begonias have appealing foliage and bloom in late summer.

• Begonias with a shrub-like growth habit include Begonia fuchsioides, which produces pendulous, tubular flowers that resemble fuchsias.

These are only a few of the many available begonia plant varieties. Begonias are a versatile and well-liked choice for both indoor and outdoor horticulture, as each variety possesses distinctive characteristics.

Selecting The Ideal Location

It is crucial for the overall health and growth of your begonia plants that you choose the ideal location for them.

Depending on the variety of begonia you are cultivating, whether they are indoor or outdoor plants, and the local climate, the optimal location can vary.

Here are some general guidelines to consider when deciding where to plant your begonias:

Landscape Begonias:

• Most begonias prefer indirect or filtered light. Avoid placing them in direct sunlight, particularly during the day's hottest hours, as this can cause their leaves to burn. Morning sun or dappled shade is usually optimal for outdoor begonias.

- Begonias require well-draining soil to prevent their roots from becoming waterlogged. Add organic matter to the soil to enhance its drainage and fertility.

- Temperature: Begonias are typically cold-sensitive. Plant them outdoors in the spring after the risk of frost has passed, and consider bringing them indoors or providing protection if the temperature drops too low.

- While begonias prefer a consistently moist environment, they dislike resting in soggy soil. Ensure that the planting area has adequate drainage.

• Shelter: If you reside in an area with strong winds, consider planting begonias in a slightly sheltered location to protect them from wind damage.

Household Begonias:

• Different begonia varieties have varying light requirements. Rex begonias favor indirect, intense light, whereas some flowering begonias can tolerate lower light levels. Consult the maintenance instructions for your specific begonia variety before placing them.

• In general, begonias, particularly those with delicate foliage, prefer higher humidity levels. You may increase humidity by misting the plants, utilizing a humidity tray, or positioning a compact humidifier nearby.

• Temperature: Indoor begonias prosper between 65 and 75 degrees Fahrenheit (18 and 24 degrees Celsius). During the winter, avoid exposing them to drafts, extreme temperature fluctuations, and chilly windows.

• Choose containers with drainage openings in order to prevent waterlogging. Use potting soil that is well-draining and suited to the type of begonia you are cultivating.

• Placement: Place indoor begonias near windows with appropriate light levels. If you are uncertain about the light intensity, consider rotating the containers frequently to promote uniform growth.

• Keep begonias away from sources of direct heat, such as radiators and heating vents, as excessive heat can exhaust the plants.

Always refer to the care instructions for the specific variety of begonia you are cultivating. In addition, by attentively observing your plants and monitoring their reaction to their current location, you can make necessary adjustments.

CHAPTER TWO
Soil And Containers

Choosing the proper soil and potting mix is crucial for the healthy development of begonia plants. Different varieties of begonias have varying soil preferences, but there are some general guidelines you can follow when it comes to soil type and potting.

Terrain Type:

• Begonias prefer well-draining soil that allows excess water to escape without difficulty. Soil saturated with water can cause root decay and other problems. By adding perlite, vermiculite, or coarse sand to your potting mix, you can create a soil mixture with excellent drainage.

• Organic Matter: Adding organic matter to the soil, such as compost or peat moss, can enhance its structure, water retention capacity, and nutrient content.

• Level of pH: Begonias prefer mildly acidic to neutral soil (pH between 6.0 and 7.0). You can evaluate the pH of your soil and make any necessary adjustments.

Growing Medium:

• You can find pre-made potting mixes labeled "African violets" or "houseplants" that are appropriate for a variety of begonias. Typically, these mixtures include peat moss, perlite, and other components.

• If you want to construct your own mix, consider mixing peat moss, perlite, and a high-quality potting soil in equal parts. This will ensure adequate drainage and ventilation.

• Additives: Depending on the variety of begonia, you may add additional components to your mixture. For instance, adding sand to the mix when growing tuberous begonias can enhance drainage for the tubers.

Selecting a Kettle:

• Choose containers with drainage openings to allow excess water to escape. This prevents root rot caused by water accumulating at the bottom of the container.

• Select a container that can accommodate the begonia's root system. Typically, the diameter of the container should be 1 to 2 inches larger than the root ball. In general, begonias prefer slightly constrained conditions to excessive container space.

• Material: Use plastic, clay, or ceramic containers that retain moisture well and allow for adequate aeration.

Fermentation Procedure:

• Add a layer of small pebbles or pottery shards to the bottom of the container to enhance drainage.

• Add Soil: Fill the container with the proper potting soil, leaving enough room at the top for irrigation.

• Planting: Remove the begonia plant carefully from its nursery container and position it in the center of the planter. Fill in the remaining space around the plant with additional potting soil, pressing gently to secure the plant.

• After repotting, thoroughly water the plant to consolidate the soil. Ensure that excess water escapes from the pot's bottom.

Different types of begonias may have specific requirements, so it's always a good idea to research the variety you're cultivating to ensure you're providing the optimal soil and potting conditions.

Watering Methods And Frequency

Proper watering is essential for the health and growth of begonias. Appropriate watering techniques can prevent problems such as root decay and promote the growth of your begonias. Here are guidelines for begonia irrigation frequency and methods:

Landscape Begonias:

• Begonias favor dependably moist, but not soggy, soil. Check the soil's moisture content by inserting your finger approximately one inch into the soil. If it feels dried, it's time to water.

• Frequency of irrigation: The frequency of irrigation depends on variables such as temperature, relative humidity, and soil drainage. During the summer, you may need to irrigate your plants more frequently. In general, water outdoor begonias when the upper inch of soil becomes dry to the touch.

• Morning Watering: Watering in the morning permits superfluous moisture to evaporate during the course of the day, thereby reducing the risk of fungal diseases. Avoid watering in the late afternoon or evening, as damp foliage can promote disease growth overnight.

Household Begonias:

• Indoor begonias must also be maintained in consistently moist soil, but care must be taken not to overwater. As described previously, determine the soil's moisture content using the finger method.

• Size of Container and Drainage: The size of the container and the quality of the drainage can influence the frequency with which you must water indoor begonias. Smaller pots dry out more quickly than larger ones, which retain moisture for extended durations.

• Indoor environments can be arid at times, particularly during the heating season. Consider using a humidity tray, misting the foliage, or placing a humidifier nearby to increase humidity levels for your begonias.

- Bottom Watering: Place the container in a saucer or water tray and allow the plant to absorb water through the drainage openings. This method prevents water from pooling on the foliage, thereby decreasing the likelihood of fungal problems.

- Top-Watering: When top-watering, moisten the soil immediately around the plant's base. To prevent disease, avoid splashing water on foliage. Water gently and uniformly until water begins to drain from the bottom of the container.

• Avoid Watering from Above: If possible, avoid watering indoor begonias from above, especially those with delicate foliage. The accumulation of water droplets on foliage as a result of overhead watering may result in fungal problems.

• Use Water at Room Temperature: Cold water can startle begonia roots. Utilize water at room temperature to irrigate your plants.

Adapting Watering to the Environment:

• Keep in mind that the frequency of watering can differ depending on the begonia variety, the season, and the local climate. Begonias may require less water during chilly months and periods of slower growth. Always monitor the moisture content of the soil and adjust your irrigation schedule accordingly.

• Observing and responding to the requirements of your plants is essential for effective watering. Begonias are more tolerant of transient dryness than constant soggy soil, so it is preferable to slightly overwater than to underwater.

• Fertilizing begonias is a crucial part of their maintenance, as it provides the nutrients necessary for healthy growth and vibrant blooms. However, excessive fertilization can cause issues, so it is essential to adhere to appropriate fertilization guidelines.

Here is how to effectively fertilize your begonias:

1. Select the Appropriate Fertilizer:

• Balanced Fertilizer: Choose a balanced, water-soluble fertilizer with proportions of nitrogen (N), phosphorus (P), and potassium (K) that are similar or identical. This formulation could be 10-10-10 or 20-20-20. The optimal ratio promotes overall development and flowering.

• Slow-Release Fertilizer: As an alternative, you can use slow-release granular fertilizers, which release nutrients progressively over time. These are particularly useful for outdoor begonias.

2. Planting Schedule:

• Outdoor Begonias: Fertilize your outdoor begonias every 4-6 weeks during the growing season (spring to early autumn). Avoid fertilizing during the season of dormancy.

- Indoor Begonias: During the blossoming season, indoor begonias also benefit from regular fertilization. Fertilize them every four to six weeks from spring to early autumn.

3. Application Procedures:

- Water-Soluble Fertilizer: In accordance with the manufacturer's instructions, dissolve the water-soluble fertilizer in water. Avoid contact with the foliage when applying the diluted solution to the soil. Always moisten the plant after fertilizing to ensure an even distribution of nutrients.

• Slow-Release Fertilizer: For slow-release fertilizer application rates, follow the manufacturer's instructions. Typically, the granules are scattered on the soil's surface and faintly mixed in. After that, water the plant.

4. Do not over-fertilize:

• Begonias are sensitive to overfertilization. An excess of fertilizer can cause soil salinization, root injury, and diminished flowering.

- Yellowing leaves, burnt margins, and stunted growth may be the result of overfertilization. If this occurs, leach the soil by watering the plant vigorously to flush away excess salts.

5. Personalized Fertilization:

- Certain begonia varieties have specific nutrient requirements. To encourage the development of blooms, begonias may benefit from slightly higher phosphorus content. Consult the care instructions for your specific begonia variety to customize your fertilization strategy.

6. Additional Guidance:

• During the winter months, when begonias typically enter a period of sluggish growth, reduce or cease fertilization.

• Always adhere to the application rates recommended on fertilizer packaging. Not always is more better.

• You should thoroughly moisten your begonias a day or two before fertilizing. Fertilizing a soil that is too desiccated may place stress on the plant's roots.

- Begonias grown outdoors may benefit from a layer of compost or organic mulch, which can release nutrients slowly as they decompose.

By adhering to a consistent and well-balanced fertilization schedule, you can ensure that your begonias receive the nutrients they require to flourish and produce attractive foliage and flowers.

CHAPTER THREE
Cutbacks And Deadheading

Pruning and deadheading are essential begonia maintenance duties that promote healthy growth, maintain a neat appearance, and stimulate abundant flowering. Here's how to prune and deadhead your begonias properly:

During pruning:

• Regular pinching or snipping of juvenile shoot tips promotes branching and a bushier growth habit. This is especially beneficial for bedding plants and begonias with fibrous roots.

• Regularly inspect your begonias for any deceased, yellowed, or diseased leaves and stems and remove them. Utilizing clean, pointed pruning shears, prune them back to healthy tissue. This aids in preventing the transmission of diseases and insects.

• Depending on the variety of begonia, it may be necessary to prune for shape and size control. If your begonia is becoming too lanky or unruly, prune the stems to promote compact growth.

• Flowers that have faded or died can be removed to encourage the plant to devote more energy to generating new blooms rather than seeds.

Planning for the future:

The process of deadheading entails removing spent or wilted blooms from a plant. This practice encourages the plant to produce new blossoms and extends the duration of flowering. Here's how to remove begonia deadheads:

• Check your begonias regularly for faded blooms and remove them. Just above a set of healthy leaves or nodes, remove faded flowers with your fingertips or a pair of small scissors. This prevents the development of seeds and redirects the plant's energy towards the production of new blossoms.

• Some begonias, especially those with flower clusters, can benefit from selective deadheading. Instead of removing entire flower stems, remove individual wilted blooms to maintain a more uniform display of color.

• Before deadheading, ensure that your pruning instruments are clean and sharp. This aids in the prevention of disease transmission and assures clean cuts.

Pruning Advice:

• Begonias are typically forgiving regarding pruning. If you are uncertain about how much to prune, you can begin by removing fewer branches and add more as necessary.

• Remember that various varieties of begonias have distinct growth and flowering patterns. Research the specific variety you are cultivating to determine its pruning requirements.

• The optimal time for significant pruning is typically during the active growing season, which for most begonia varieties is spring through summer.

Deadheading Advice:

• Regularly remove spent flowers throughout the blossoming season to maintain a tidier appearance and promote continued blooming.

• Remove withered flowers with care so as not to harm the plant's healthy parts.

• Certain types of begonias, such as tuberous begonias, benefit from having their spent flower stalks removed entirely. This permits the plant to concentrate on conserving energy in the tubers for the following season.

By employing appropriate pruning and deadheading techniques, you can help your begonias flourish, preserve their appearance, and produce an extended period of vibrant blooms.

Propagation Techniques

There are several methods for propagating begonias, depending on the variety of begonia and the desired outcome. Here are some common methods for propagating begonias:

1. Leaf Trimmings:

• Numerous varieties of begonias, including rex, cane, and rhizomatous begonias, are suitable for this method.

• Select a robust leaf with an attached stem. Remove the leaf and a portion of its stem.

• Soak the sliced end in a hormone that promotes rooting (optional but helpful).

• Plant the leaf stem in a well-draining potting mix, leaving the leaf exposed and submerging the cut end.

• Place the cutting in an environment that is warm, humid,

and illuminated by indirect, brilliant light. Maintain consistent soil moisture.

• After several weeks, roots should develop and new plantlets will emerge from the base of the leaf.

2. Rhizome Sectioning:

• Rhizomatous begonias, which develop from thick, horizontal stems known as rhizomes, are suitable for this method.

• Gently remove the plant from its container and separate the rhizomes with attached roots.

• Each section should contain robust roots and a minimum of one growing point (shoot).

• Replant the divided sections in individual containers containing soil that drains well.

• Water the divisions and maintain them in a warm, moist environment until new growth emerges.

3. Stem Reductions:

• This technique is frequently employed for cane begonias.

• Take a robust 3- to 4-inch-long stem cutting with multiple nodes (points where leaves emerge).

• Eliminate the lower leaves, leaving only a few at the summit.

• Soak the severed end in rooting hormone and plant it in a potting mix with excellent drainage.

• Maintain the cutting in a warm, moist environment with indirect, brilliant light.

• Regularly water the cutting and mist its foliage to maintain humidity.

• Within a few weeks, roots should develop, and new growth will indicate successful rooting.

4. Tuber Department:

• This procedure is unique to tuberous begonias.

• After the growing season, when the plant is inert, remove the tubers with care.

• Separate the tubers carefully, ensuring that each section has a healthy growth bud or eye.

• Allow the divided tubers to air-dry for a few days so that any cuts or wounds can recover.

• Replant the tuber sections in well-draining soil, partially concealing them with their growth buds facing upward.

• Lightly water the tubers and store them in a calm, dry location until new growth emerges.

5. Seed Reproduction:

• Begonias can be grown from seedlings, but this requires additional time and attention.

• Sow begonia seeds on the surface of a potting mixture with excellent drainage and gently press them down.

• Begonia seeds require light to germinate; therefore, cover them with a thin layer of vermiculite or fine soil.

• Create a humid environment by misting the surface and wrapping the container in plastic wrap.

• Maintain a warm temperature and brilliant, indirect lighting in the container.

• Germination can take several weeks to months; once seedlings have developed true leaves, they can be transplanted into individual containers.

Different types of begonia have distinct propagation requirements, so it is essential to conduct research and adhere to the specific instructions for the variety you are propagating. Propagation requires patience, as it may take time for new plants to establish and thrive.

CHAPTER FOUR
Pest And Disease Control

Managing pests and diseases is essential for keeping your begonias healthy and flourishing. Begonias can be susceptible to a variety of pests and diseases, so it is essential to routinely inspect your plants and take corrective measures at the first sign of trouble. The following are prevalent pests and diseases that affect begonias, as well as management strategies:

Frequent pests:

1. Aphids: These tiny insects congregate on the undersides of foliage and feed on plant juices, resulting in distorted growth and honeydew accumulation.

• Management: Use a vigorous water stream, insecticidal soap or neem oil, or introduce natural predators such as ladybugs.

2. These microscopic parasites are responsible for stippled leaves and webs. They thrive in arid environments.

• Increase humidity, mist the leaves frequently, isolate afflicted plants, and apply insecticidal soap or neem oil for management.

3. Mealybugs are tiny, white insects that resemble cottony aggregates on plant components. They take in sap and expel fructose.

• Control: Remove them manually, spot-treat with cotton bathed in rubbing alcohol, or use insecticidal soap.

4. Whiteflies are small, flying insects that congregate on leaves and feed on sap, causing leaves to yellow and wilt.

• Use yellow adhesive traps, introduce natural predators, or apply insecticidal soap for management.

5. These insects feed on plant fluids by attaching themselves to leaves and stems. They resemble tiny, round or oval lumps.

• Management: manually eliminate them or use insecticidal soap.

Common Ailments:

1. Granular Mildew: This fungal disease affects the health and appearance of leaves by causing a white, granular coating.

• Management: Increase airflow, avoid overhead watering, and administer fungicide sprays as necessary.

2. Botrytis Blight (Gray Mold): This disease causes foliage and flowers to develop a grayish mold. It frequently flourishes in humid environments.

• Management: Increase air circulation, separate plants, removes diseased plant parts, and administers fungicides.

3. Leaf patches are dark or discolored patches that appear on leaves. They can be caused by a variety of fungi or bacteria.

• Management consists of removing infected foliage, avoiding overhead watering, and applying fungicides as needed.

4. Root Rot: Root rot is caused by excessively moist soil and can result in leaves turning yellow and plant death.

• Management: Ensure well-draining soil, permit the soil to evaporate slightly between waterings, and prevent waterlogging.

Precautionary Measures:

• Provide proper development conditions, including adequate light, humidity, and airflow.

• Quarantine: Isolate new plants for several weeks prior to introducing them to your collection in order to prevent the spread of pests and diseases.

• Cleanliness: Remove fallen leaves and detritus from around your plants on a regular basis to reduce pest and disease hiding places.

• Avoid overwatering, which can contribute to fungal problems, and water the soil rather than the plant's foliage.

• Adequate Spacing: Avoid overcrowding your plants, as this can reduce airflow and increase the likelihood of disease.

You can effectively manage these issues and maintain the health and beauty of your begonias by maintaining vigilance, adhering to good cultural practices, and taking prompt action upon spotting any signs of pests or diseases.

Internal And External Cultivation

Begonias can be grown both indoors and outdoors; the method you employ will depend on the type of begonia you're cultivating and the local climate. Here is a breakdown of indoor and outdoor:

1. Begonia cultivation:

Indoor Agriculture:

• Place begonias indoors in indirect, brilliant light. Different varieties of begonias have varying light requirements; therefore, you should research the specific variety you intend to cultivate.

• Avoid exposing begonias to direct sunlight, particularly during the hottest portions of the day, as this can cause their leaves to burn.

2. The temperature is:

• For the majority of begonias, keep indoor temperatures between 65°F and 75°F (18°C and 24°C).

• During the winter, avoid exposing begonias to drafts, extreme temperature fluctuations, and chilly windows.

3. Relative humidity:

• In general, begonias prefer higher humidity levels. Mist the plants, use a humidity tray, or place a humidifier nearby to increase humidity.

4. The act of watering:

• When the top inch of soil is dried to the touch, water your indoor begonias.

• Use water at room temperature and avoid overwatering to avoid root decay.

5. Compost and Containers:

• Choose well-draining potting mixes suitable for the specific variety of begonia you're growing.

• To ensure appropriate water drainage, choose containers with drainage holes.

6. To fertilize:

• Fertilize indoor begonias every 4 to 6 weeks with balanced, water-soluble fertilizers during the growing season.

• Follow the manufacturer's application rate recommendations.

7. Defoliation and Deadheading:

• Regularly prune and remove spent flowers to maintain the plant's form and encourage flowering.

• To prevent pests and diseases, you must remove deceased or diseased plants.

Outdoor Production:

• Depending on the variety, outdoor begonias have varying light requirements. Others can tolerate more sunlight while others prefer partial shade.

• Provide outdoor begonias with filtered light or morning sun.

The temperature is:

• Begonias should be planted outdoors in the spring after the threat of frost has passed. They generally flourish in temperate climates.

• During the colder months, protect them from low temperatures and weather.

The act of watering:

Be sure to water outdoor begonias when the top inch of soil feels dried to the touch. Avoid overwatering, particularly in soils with poor drainage.

Soil and Vegetation:

• Prepare a well-draining soil for begonias grown outdoors. To increase fertility, amend the soil with humus or organic matter.

• Plant begonias at the appropriate depth for their type, ensuring that they are secure without being submerged too deeply.

To fertilize:

• Fertilize outdoor begonias every 4 to 6 weeks with balanced, water-soluble fertilizers during the growing season.

• Utilize slow-release fertilizers for convenience and a constant supply of nutrients.

Pest and Disease Control:

• Regularly inspect outdoor begonias for parasites and diseases, and take prompt action if problems arise.

Defoliation and Deadheading:

• Similar to indoor begonias, outdoor begonias benefit from routine pruning and deadheading in order to promote healthy growth and flowering.

Winter Upkeep:

Some outdoor begonias, such as tuberous begonias, require frost protection during the winter months. During the quiescent period, lift the tubers and store them indoors.

Remember that various begonia varieties have distinct maintenance requirements. Always refer to the specific care instructions for the type of begonia you are cultivating to ensure optimal growth, whether indoors or outdoors.

CHAPTER FIVE
Container Horticulture With Begonias

Container gardening with begonias is an excellent way to enjoy these lovely plants on terraces, balconies, and even indoors. Begonias offer a variety of hues, textures, and shapes that can enhance the aesthetics of your outdoor or indoor spaces. Here is how to construct a successful begonia container garden:

1. Select the Appropriate Begonia Varieties:

• Select begonia varieties that thrive in containers. Popular options include fibrous-rooted begonias, tuberous begonias, and rex begonias.

• Consider the lighting conditions of your selected location and select begonias with light requirements that correspond to those conditions.

2. Container Choosing:

• Select containers with drainage openings to prevent water accumulation.

• Containers should be proportional to the variety of begonia being cultivated. A container with a diameter of 10 to 14 inches works well for the majority of begonias.

3. Growing Medium:

• Use a potting mix that is well-draining and appropriate for the type of begonia you are cultivating. Mixtures designated "African violets" or "houseplants" are frequently appropriate.

• If you are cultivating tuberous begonias, consider incorporating grit into the potting mixture to improve drainage.

4. The act of planting:

• Fill the container with potting soil, leaving room for irrigation.

• Gently remove the begonia from its nursery container and position it in the center of the pot. Ensure the root ball is flush with the soil's surface.

• Fill in the sides with additional potting soil, gingerly pressing it around the plant to secure it.

5. The act of watering:

• After planting, thoroughly water the begonia to consolidate the soil and eliminate air pockets.

• Water when the top inch of soil becomes dried to the touch. To prevent waterlogging, ensure that excess water can escape through the drainage openings.

6. Located at:

• Select a location that provides the ideal lighting conditions for the begonia variety you are cultivating. For instance, fibrous-rooted begonias prefer filtered light, whereas tuberous-rooted begonias can tolerate greater exposure to sunlight.

7. To fertilize:

• Fertilize your container-grown begonias every 4 to 6 weeks during the growing season with a balanced, water-soluble fertilizer.

8. The upkeep of:

• Regularly remove faded blooms to promote continuous flowering.

• Monitor your begonias for parasites and diseases, and take corrective action as necessary.

• Prune lanky growth to promote denser growth.

• After the growing season, allow tuberous begonias to go dormant by reducing irrigation and removing the foliage.

9. Concept and Aesthetics:

• Combine various begonia varieties to create aesthetically pleasing containers.

• Combine begonias with complementary plants such as ferns, ivy, or trailing tendrils for added texture and visual appeal.

Container gardening with begonias enables you to add color and attractiveness to small spaces and create a verdant environment despite having limited garden space.

Your begonias can flourish and provide a stunning display throughout the growing season if you provide them with the appropriate care and attention.

Managing Anxiety And Transplant Shock

In order for your begonias to successfully adapt to a new environment or container, it is essential that they are able to withstand tension and transplant shock.

Both outdoor and indoor begonias are susceptible to stress and trauma when they are transplanted or moved.

Here's how you can assist your begonias in surviving these conditions:

1. Organ Transplant Shock:

• When a plant is relocated to a new location or repotted, transplant shock occurs.

Begonias are susceptible to transplant shock, particularly if they have not been acclimated correctly. Here are some ways to reduce transplant shock:

- Prepare the New Container: Ensure that the new container is of the correct dimensions and containsOricum holes. Fill it with the correct potting soil for the specific type of begonia.

- Water Prior to Transplanting: Water the begonia thoroughly one to two days prior to transplanting. This ensures the plant is adequately hydrated and under less stress throughout the procedure.

- Transplant During milder Hours: Whenever possible, transplant during the day's milder hours, such as the Public, the, and the. This reduces heat-related tension.

• Gentle Handling: When transplanting begonias, handle them with care to avoid damaging their roots or stems.

• Acclimation: If you are moving your begonia from indoors to outdoors (or vice versa), progressively acclimate it to the new environment by placing it in a shaded or protected location for a few hours per day and increasing its exposure to sunlight.

• Irrigation Following Transplanting: Irrigate the begonia immediately after transplanting to help stabilize the soil and reduce stress. Make sure water reaches the root zone.

Avoid fertilizing immediately after transplanting to reduce stress. Before introducing additional nutrients, allow the plant some time to adapt.

2. Coping with Tension:

Various factors, including changes in the environment, lighting, humidity, temperature, and water availability, can induce stress in begonias. How to assist your begonias in coping with stress:

• Maintain a consistent care routine, including regular irrigation, adequate lighting, and adequate humidity levels.

• Prevent Abrupt Changes: Begonias are sensitive to abrupt changes. Introduce them to novel conditions gradually to reduce stress.

• Pruning: Remove damaged or stressed foliage to refocus the plant's energy on healthy growth.

• Humidity: Begonias appreciate higher levels of humidity. Use a humidity tray or frequently mist the leaves to increase humidity around the plant if the air is too dry.

• Temperature: Maintain the optimal temperature range for your specific begonia variety. Temperature fluctuations can cause plant stress.

• While begonias prefer dependably moist soil, overwatering can cause stress and root rot. Ensure proper drainage and only water when the top inch of soil is dried to the touch.

• Be patient when introducing begonias to new environmental conditions. They might require some time to adapt and recover from tension.

By taking these measures, you can lessen the effects of transplant shock and assist your begonias in coping with stress, thereby promoting their healthy growth and well-being.

Implementing Begonias In Landscape Design

Begonias can add a splash of color, texture, and visual interest to your outdoor spaces when used in landscaping design.

Begonias offer versatile alternatives for enhancing the landscape, whether you're working with garden beds, borders, containers, or hanging baskets. Here are some suggestions for using begonias in your landscape design.

1. Borders and Garden Beds:

• Colorful Mass Plantings: Plant begonias in clusters or rows to produce arresting color displays. Choose a single hue or a combination of hues for a vibrant effect.

• Begonias can be used to edge garden plots and borders. Their dense growth and vibrant flowers can create a well-defined border.

• Mixed Plantings: Combine begonias with other floral plants, foliage plants, and ornamental grasses to create arrangements that are diverse and visually appealing.

• Consider pairing begonias with plants that have foliage with contrasting colors, shapes, and textures to create dynamic and intriguing combinations.

2. Container Plants:

• Containers: Use begonias as the focal point or centerpiece of your container gardens. Choose containers that complement the begonias' colors and designs.

• Mix and match: Combine various begonia varieties in the same container to create a dazzling array of colors and shapes. Use trailing or filler plants to add texture to a landscape.

• Vertical Gardens: Utilize hanging containers, wall planters, or trellises to incorporate begonias into vertical gardens. This maximizes space and gives your landscape dimension.

3. Window Boxes and Hanging Baskets:

• Begonias with Trailing Habits: Many begonia varieties have trailing habits, making them ideal for hanging containers and window boxes. Their cascading growth makes for an attractive display.

• Color Coordination: To create a harmonious appearance, coordinate begonia colors with the exterior colors of your home or outdoor space.

4. Covered Gardens:

• Begonias flourish in areas that are shaded by trees. Plant them beneath trees, along paths, or in other areas with limited direct sunlight.

• Combine begonias with shade-loving ferns, hostas, and other foliage plants to create a luxuriant and textural shade garden.

5. Seasonal Decorations:

• Seasonal Beds: Begonias can be used to create seasonal beds by varying their colors and variants according to the season.

• Autumn and Winter Displays: Even when not in bloom, certain begonia varieties offer colorful foliage that adds visual appeal to autumn and winter displays.

6. Focus Areas:

• Centerpiece Beds: Designate a focal point bed in which begonias are featured prominently. Utilize their vivid hues and luxuriant foliage to attract attention.

7. Features of Water:

• Around Ponds and Fountains: Begonias lend color and vibrancy to these tranquil spaces when planted around water features.

Consider the specific growing requirements of the begonia varieties you select, and adapt your design accordingly.

Whether you're striving for a formal, structured layout or a more natural, relaxed design, begonias provide a variety of options for enhancing your landscaping and creating a beautiful outdoor oasis.

CHAPTER SIX
Begonia Hybridization And New Developments

Begonia hybridization is a fascinating and inventive aspect of horticulture involving the cross-breeding of various begonia species and cultivars to produce new and distinctive cultivars.

Plant breeders can use hybridization to produce begonias with enhanced color, size, shape, and disease resistance by combining desirable traits from multiple begonia species.

Here's a look at the hybridization and innovation of begonias:

1. Objectives of Hybridization:

• Color Enhancement: Breeders can intensify and modify the colors of begonia blooms, generating new and vibrant hues that do not necessarily exist in nature.

• Size and Shape: Hybridization can result in begonias with larger blossoms, more compact growth habits, and distinctive flower shapes.

• Breeders can experiment with various textures, patterns, and hues of foliage, resulting in begonias with striking foliage.

• Breeders can produce begonias that are more resistant to common parasites and diseases by selecting for disease-resistant characteristics.

• Climate Adaptation: Hybridization can result in begonias that are better adapted to particular growing conditions, such as extreme heat, cold, or humidity.

2. Breeding Strategies:

• Begonia hybridization requires transferring pollen manually from the stamen (male reproductive structure) of one begonia flower to the stigma (female reproductive structure) of another flower.

• Breeders meticulously select parent plants with the desired characteristics. This may involve selecting one plant based on its floral color and another based on its growth habit.

• Controlled Pollination: Breeders regulate the pollination process to ensure the transmission of the desired characteristics. By covering flowers with protective sacks, they prevent unwanted natural pollination.

3. Developments in Begonia Hybridization:

• Tissue Culture: Tissue culture techniques allow breeders to proliferate begonias from small plant tissue samples in a rapid manner. This technique expedites the spread of novel hybrids.

• Genetic Manipulation: Developments in genetic engineering may result in innovative hybrids with specific traits introduced or altered at the genetic level.

• Stress Tolerance: As concerns about climate change increase, breeders may concentrate on creating begonias that are more tolerant of fluctuating environmental conditions.

• Breeders can experiment with new flower shapes, such as double blossoms or unusual petal arrangements.

- Breeders may also consider developing hybrids that require less water or are more resistant to parasites, thereby contributing to sustainable gardening practices.

4. Societies of Horticulturists and Hybridization:

- Numerous horticultural societies and botanical gardens engage in begonia hybridization in order to preserve uncommon species, develop new cultivars, and advance scientific knowledge.

5. Collaborative Initiatives:

•   Botanical institutions, plant breeders, and enthusiasts exchange knowledge, genetic resources, and techniques, thereby contributing to the ongoing innovation in begonia hybridization.

Begonia hybridization is a fascinating field that combines science and art, resulting in an endless stream of new begonia varieties that delight gardeners and collectors.

These hybrids demonstrate the ingenuity of horticulturists while contributing to the diversity and attractiveness of the plant kingdom.

The Conclusion

With their astounding variety of colors, shapes, and growth behaviors, begonias offer gardeners and enthusiasts a universe of opportunities. Begonias always add beauty and sophistication to any space, whether they are grown indoors, outdoors, in containers, or as part of intricate landscaping designs. Begonias are captivating and versatile, from their exquisite flowers to their intricate foliage.

You can witness the remarkable transformation of begonias from tiny seeds, cuttings, or tubers into thriving, vibrant plants by providing them with attentive care, nurturing, and knowledge of their specific requirements.

The journey includes selecting the ideal location, providing optimal light, water, and nutrients, and diligently managing pests and diseases. You will learn to anticipate their growth, flowering cycles, and unique characteristics as you immerse yourself in their world.

Incorporating begonias into your landscape design not only adds aesthetic appeal, but also provides a blank canvas for your imagination. Begonias are a versatile medium for expressing your personal style and vision, whether you're looking to create a harmonious color palette, introduce focal points, or experiment with textural contrasts.

In addition, the world of begonia hybridization and innovation is evidence of human ingenuity and the natural marvels of plant genetics.

Plant breeders continue to stretch the boundaries, creating hybrids that astonish with their colors, sizes, and forms. These endeavors demonstrate our capacity to harness nature's majesty while preserving its delicate equilibrium, bridging tradition and modern science.

In conclusion, begonias are more than just plants; they are living artworks that inspire, delight, and connect us to the natural world's miracles. Whether you are a seasoned gardener or a novice, growing begonias is a journey filled with pleasure, learning, and a profound appreciation for the beauty that nature so generously bestows upon us.

Consequently, whether you are tending to indoor pots, designing expansive gardens, or engaging in the world of hybridization, begonias serve as a reminder of the extraordinary harmony between human creativity and the beauty of the plant kingdom.

THE END

Printed in Great Britain
by Amazon

34558191R00059